It's Okay
Poetic Memoirs

By
Mary Rogers-Grantham

It's Okay: Poetic Memoirs by Mary Rogers-Grantham
Copyright © 2015 by Mary Rogers-Grantham

It's Okay: Poetic Memoirs by Mary Rogers-Grantham
34p. ill. cm.
ISBN 978-0-9793362-0-1

All Rights Reserved. No part of this book may be reproduced, stored in a retrieval system, or transmitted in any form or by any means, electronic, mechanical, photocopying, recording, or otherwise, without permission in writing from MRK Publishing

MRK Publishing
PO Box 353431
Palm Coast, FL 32135-3431

To Mother and Daddy, the lighthouse of my life.

Table Of Contents

Hush. Hear the Silence	3
The Storybook Heart	4
Change	6
Classic Waves of Peace	7
Message in the Melody	8
Painting Images	9
Wanting	10
He Made the Universe	12
Spring Play	13
Petals	14
Matters of Nature	15
Annals	17
Unconditional Grounds	18
Mud Pies	19
Literacy in the Barnyard	20
Breakfast Delights	21
Salvaged Comforts	22
What's the Matter	24
About the Author	26

OPENING
Let your thoughts flow like river streams.
Then, let them ebb on tidal pages.

Hush. Hear the Silence.

Silence is a giver, not a beggar.
It offers peace and comfort.
It doesn't attempt to out-talk anyone.
It doesn't even attempt to compete with anyone.
Silence never changes.
It is the same as yesterday.
It is the same today.
It will be the same tomorrow.
Let it shower you with peace
and blanket you with comfort.
Silence offers wisdom.
Hush.

The Storybook Heart

Open the cover and notice the author's name, yours.
Turn the page and note the copyright date, your birth.
Look further. You'll discover all your rights are reserved.
Read the table of contents, the chapters of your life.
Turn the page. Read the introduction, the preface of your life.
Turn another page and read a list of names, the contributors to the story of your life.

Humble yourself. Begin a lifetime.

TRANSFORMATIONS
I used to be a pebble, but now I'm a rock.

Change

begins with self.

Researching, reflecting

and remodeling

the person within.

Discovering, uncovering,

and disclosing

 self-worth, values

and morals.

Classic Waves of Peace

I was up early, as usual, a few minutes past 5 a.m.
The normal racing behaviors of my mind were silenced
by many positive thoughts. So, I let the quietness
of the morning embrace me.
It felt good, like moments spent in health spas,
rejuvenating some muscles, encouraging
others to relax and rest in the shadows.
I prepared breakfast for my Cocker Spaniel, Norm
and my Persian cat, Socky, and let the plans for the day have
their way.

They spoke fluently about their agenda, and I received
them without resistance, without tug of war.
Classical music on the radio played ever so softly,
a perfect background for the tranquil morning.
Those artists from long ago, must have sensed
the need to set the stage for this special time in my day,
the music seemed to have been written just for me.
They must have known when I'd be up that day,
for each note was in tune with its breaking.
So, I rode the tides of the classics
and dared myself to look at the past.

Clothed in the life jacket of grace,
I welcomed gentle waves of peace.

Message in the Melody

I remember when
I was a ***wanna' be soprano***.
I tried.
I remember when
I chose to be an ***alterin' alto***.
I tried.
Now I am a ***strugglin' tenor.***
Still, I try.

Painting Images

Artists do it.
They paint winter landscapes, autumn scenes,
spring settings and summer sights.
Seizing a moment in time and place,
they capture the beauty they perceive
in images of people, places
and things of interest.
Simplicities and complexities.
They paint what they know.
They paint what they see.
Skeptics do it.
They use words to paint the environment
they perceive as a threat to their well being.
Making meaning of their perceptions,
they paint stirring images of people,
places and things
that intimidate them.
Fears and doubts.
They paint what they don't know.
They paint what they don't see.

Wanting

Too many years
gone dormant,
too many days
fast asleep,
too much time
washed downstream.
Turbulent winters
frozen in place,
beautiful springs
silenced by haze,
aggressive summers
fermented in dampness,
tepid autumns
abandoned to images.
Wanting.

NATURE MATTERS
In the midst of everything else in the world, nature matters.

He Made the Universe

He made the universe.
Fishes giggling about life
in the rivers, the oceans and the seas;
fowl risking flight through
the endless air that surrounds them;
animals daring to move freely within their means;
plant life tickling the earth's soil with its growth.
They are symbols of the cost of freedom
that comes when total trust
is put into action.
Like the fishes, let's giggle
about life in the universe.
Like the fowl, let's risk
our dreams by taking flight.
Like the animals, let's dare
to move freely, but with purpose.
Like the plant life, let's humor Him
by tickling our faith.
For, He made the universe.

Spring Play

Winter had just lifted the weight of its arctic curtain
exposing a barren walnut tree just outside the fence
that divided the backyard from the field.
Its giant trunk sat atop the earth,
sharing a piece of its brown and green space.
While modeling a never ending waistline,
it boasted bountiful muscled limbs.
Some appeared to reach upward
as if grasping for the stars.
Others appeared to sprawl outward.
Certain that winter company was gone, they began
to dress. Mother Nature clothed them in tender green leaves
that would soon flirt with the sun. And then she dabbed them
with fragrant buds that would blossom in the arms
of quiet breezes. Virgin, carefree blooms stared
tenderly into the eyes of soft breezes.
Warmed by day and cooled by night,
they begged the moments to never end.
Nature's vigilant eyes witnessed
the annual spring play staged by winter's flight.

A barren walnut tree,
limbs, leaves, buds,
blossoms and soft breezes;
a love story,
walnuts.

Petals

Eyes behold their appearance
while minds study their shape, and
spirits admire their grace.
They wave from the kiss of a breeze,
cradle the dews of a spring morning,
and are caressed by raindrops after a shower.
They sun in the still of a summer day,
offer comfort to insects that come to visit,
befriend butterflies that take rest from flight
or come to take pleasure in their pollen.
They appear to be committed to their season,
and patient with their visitors.
They accept a brief, fragile life
of serenity and humility
until their passing.

Matters of Nature

A blade of grass
A bug on a blade of grass
A leaf on a tree
A bug on a leaf on a tree
A flower petal
A bug on the flower petal
Gently it rests
On the blade of grass
Gently it crawls
About the leaf on the tree
Gently it explores
The back of the flower petal
Thoughts on a blade of grass
Freedom on the leaf of the tree
Wonder underneath the flower petal
A bug
A leaf
A flower petal
Nature matters.

COMING HOME
"Like dust mites that collect in abandoned places, memories collect on the window panes of the mind."

Annals

Her heart was her personal library
where she let her thoughts browse
its many shelves.
Her vacant eyes stared softly into yesterday.
A little girl remembered
Unlike clock alarms set for a certain wakening hour,
her alarms were silent and unannounced.
They mocked her sleeping breaths and painted
water colored smiles, blueprints for her tomorrows.
Satisfied with their impressive performance,
they left residual memories
then continued their sojourn.
Like proud members of a marching band,
they kept time with the silent rhythms ahead,
in tune with the confidence of their leader.
Aromas of homemade biscuits baking in the oven
She remembered the welcoming trails that zigzagged
through the farm lands and the cool wooded areas.
Each one etched with care;
tall weeds laid carefully to one side, and
briar branches pushed tenderly to the other,
signs of frequent visitors.
Deep greens, tender browns and gentle pastels,
harmonious tones coloring the miracle of life.
Memoirs of spring and summer adventures
In the heart of her personal library,
vacant eyes stared softly into yesterday,
and kept company with a trail of thoughts
that tickled her memories.

Unconditional Grounds

The grounds around the house were always friendly.
They were vulnerable to all the seasonal elements.
Spring rains played hide and seek with the new grasses.
Summer storms taunted the flower and vegetable gardens.
Autumn temperatures frolicked carelessly upon veteran soils.
Winter air challenged the dusty, gravel trails to games of scrimmage.
The grounds around the house were always friendly,
giving much and receiving all.

Mud Pies

Mornings arrived early with quiet daybreak songs.
Their gentle notes touched one eyelid, then the other.
Wakefulness stirred all five of my senses while the
the presence of unrelenting dawns reminded me
"Rise now, your playhouse awaits you."
In the midst of the early summer mornings,
my growing bare feet carried me to the backdoor
of the kitchen where I gazed upon a sleepy backyard
and a yet slumbering field, a welcoming audience.
In the silence of the early summer mornings,
while a lazy sun had breakfast with a yawning horizon,
I made mud pies in my playhouse.

Literacy in the Barnyard

We sat at the edge of the floor in the open door of the barn.
Daddy's feet rested on the ground,
mine dangled loosely beside his ankle.
I was eager for the day they would rest
flat on the ground beside his.
Outside the gate, Tansy, the milk cow,
and Daisy, the plow horse, were enjoying
hay and grains.
Daddy's gaze at them was one
of a contented father.
I picked up the book I had brought with me,
A Child's Primer, with colorful short narratives
about Baby Ray and Little Boy Blue.
I opened it and said, "Daddy, let's read."
The gentle movement of his head in my direction
was his silent confirmation, "Okay."
We began our lesson, me pointing and gliding
my right index finger underneath each word.
Gulps of air preceded his efforts to call words.
We sat at the edge of the floor in the open door of the barn
and invited each character into the barnyard to listen as we
read.

Breakfast Delights

The crack of dawn found her tickling
the bellies of her floured biscuit dough.
Like the certainty of daybreak,
she prepared them every morning
by carefully mixing her memorized recipe,
then fluffing them into their *just right* shapes.
Mother placed each mass of dough
on her favorite baking pan.
With a look of contentment,
she opened the oven door,
placed them on the rack,
and trusted a sizzling temperature
to transform them into flaky brown,
healthy, breakfast delights .

Salvaged Comforts
*—Written for my sister, "Booster's"
birthday celebration*

Teddy Bear and Dolly sprawled comfortably atop a bed made with care. They didn't seem to mind keeping company with the myriad of shapes and designs representing the pride of one family's clothing lineage.

So, they rested peacefully while a handmade quilt whispered colorful tales about the nature of its characters. Each salvaged scrap of fabric shared amusing tales about their wear to school, to work, to church and to play.

Teddy Bear and Dolly seemed amused by the rhapsody of the stories, and affected by the quiet strength and courage that emerged from each one of them. Each pair of faded pupils appeared to darken with renewal as kindred spirits continued their tireless journey in the attitude of service, still offering company to those who passed their way.

Today, one of those kindred spirits continues her journey. Fabric once adorned by her can still be seen in handmade quilts from long ago. Now and again, she revisits the sojourns of her life.

Once in a while, she shares a choice chapter from her narrative. Observe as she thoughtfully recreates humorous dramas. Listen carefully as she cleverly plants the storyline inside the plot. Pay close attention while she creates colorful characters by using meticulous details that are sure to awaken the imagination.

There are Mother and Daddy stories, Joe, Jr., Pearl Lene and Cleter Bell stories. There are Merlee stories and even her own Booster stories.

For example, there is Butlah, The Great Cucumber Picker and

Basketball on the Rocks. There are the infamous Miss Willie's Sunday School stories, not to mention her acting debut in the high school play, "The Devil's Funeral."

Like Teddy Bear and Dolly, watch and listen as a remarkable director and a natural actress bring the theater of your mind to life. Ask a living kindred spirit, who has the memory of a griot, to share some amusing tales from her memoirs of salvaged comforts.

What's the Matter?

After you were gone, I entered your room.
The lights were on.
One lone peppermint disk lay in the company
of a safety pin on the hotel notepad.
Like a toddler tugging at the hem of its mother's garment,
nostalgia attempted to gain my attention
by forcing my lips into a superficial smile.
Slowly, I walked to the end of your room
looking left, then right.
There was a reason I had gone there,
to be embraced by the remnants
of your presence, all gone now,
to touch the damp towel that dried your body
just a while ago.
A single tissue rested gently on its haunches on top of the
dresser.
An empty milk carton lay idly in a trash can
that appeared to crouch beneath the hotel's table desk.
Your room was the magnet.
My emptiness was the draw.

"Let the beginning and the closing of each chapter in this precious gift of life, always be written from the soul of your heart."

About the Author

Mary Rogers-Grantham adores family and teaching, respects nature and humanity, and enjoys writing poetry and traveling. These subjects are often presented in poetic memoirs and in other poetic forms, which have been published in several literary journals. Her poetry collections include *It's Okay: Poetic Memoirs*, *Clear Velvet*, *Under a Daylight Moon*, and *Rotating Reflections: A Poetry Trio*. Mary grew up in Southwest Arkansas and taught high school and college English in Kansas City, Missouri. She is a new Florida resident, teaches at Flagler College in St. Augustine and is working on her next poetry collection *Turn Down the Sun*.

www.ingramcontent.com/pod-product-compliance
Lightning Source LLC
Chambersburg PA
CBHW050609300426
44112CB00013B/2136